music
matters

understanding and

applying the

amazing power

of godly music

cary schmidt

First published in 2007 by Striving Together Publications, a ministry
of Lancaster Baptist Church, Lancaster, CA 93535. Striving Together
Publications is committed to providing tried, trusted, and proven
books that will further equip local churches to carry out the Great
Commission. Your comments and suggestions are valued.

Striving Together Publications
4020 E. Lancaster Blvd.
Lancaster, CA 93535
800.201.7748
www.strivingtogether.com

Cover design by Andrew Jones
Layout by Craig Parker
Edited by Amanda Michael, Sarah Michael, and Danielle Mordh
Special thanks to our proofreaders.

ISBN 978-1-59894-037-4

Printed in the United States of America

Table of Contents

Introduction

Does music matter? There is a popular Christian teaching adopted by many that says "music doesn't matter." This thought seems to promote an "anything goes" mentality and says that "God created and likes all kinds of music." Is this really true?

Before we get started examining this question, I'd like to share my heart on a few very important points.

First, this is probably one the most contentious topics in Christendom today. Music is a "hot button" with many people. Various positions and opinions on music are debated, argued, and staunchly defended. The very mention of the topic can cause an immediate spirit of defensiveness or carnality and a wide variety of unfavorable emotional responses.

Before you read on—please relax. The Bible says, "Only by pride cometh contention: but with the well advised is wisdom" (Proverbs 13:10). Let's set aside our pride and simply seek to be "well advised" on this subject.

The spirit of these pages is to reason with you. Perhaps we could learn something about music on this brief journey that we never considered before. The point of this little book is not to stir contention or controversy. It is to simply inform you of the amazing power and influence that this form of communication has upon your life. The response and choices you make as a result are between you and God.

Second, this is an intensely personal subject. Music is very much a "personal god" in modern culture. The "I want my MTV" attitude is pervasive. We often see our musical tastes as a subject of personal preference with which nobody (including God) has the right to meddle. So, while I promise not to meddle, I do ask that you open your heart to what God has to say. I believe His Word and the principles contained therein are clear. And since He owns us, let's give Him entrance into this subject. There truly is no "personal space" in our lives that should exclude God. May the "American Idol" of music not be our idol as Christians.

Third, the way music exists and permeates our culture is a relatively new phenomenon. Over the last one hundred years, technology has radically transformed the way our modern culture interacts with music. For thousands of years the human voice was the primary way that common men enjoyed music throughout the day. Beyond the voice, if you wanted to listen to music, you either had to learn to play an instrument, or be relatively close to those who could.

How different things are today! It began over one hundred years ago with the invention of the phonograph and the development of broadcast media. Music began to be thrust into a more accessible and prominent position in American culture during the twentieth century. In recent decades we've seen another quantum leap forward with the invention of portable players, cell phones, and wireless networks. I'm not saying this is all bad, but it is a significant social change of global proportions.

Bringing music from the concert halls of the nineteenth century to the ear-buds of the twenty-first century has produced numerous, massive cultural shifts that we couldn't begin to address in these brief pages. What's the point? Simply this:

Music is now pervasive in our culture, and we are a generation of experimentation when it comes to modern musical power. The phenomenon of portable, on-demand music is fairly new; and it hasn't only resulted in new technology, it has resulted in a wide variety of radical new musical styles and the accompanying "lifestyles" as well. In addition, you cannot go anywhere in modern society without being influenced by background music—it is the unseen moderator of so much of our lives, whether through TV, at a restaurant, in a grocery store, or waiting for a dental appointment.

Yet, we can't look to history to see the outcome of all this change. We can't ask "how did past generations deal with these challenges?" The Apostle Paul wasn't preaching in Philippi to kids with iPods.

Fourth, this is an intensely biblical matter. The Bible has much to say about music—its purpose, its power, and its priority in our lives. So many Christians are quick to assume that the Bible is silent regarding musical styles. This simply isn't the case.

The Bible is filled with principles—not specifics, but guidelines that should guide our decisions regarding music. Like fashion, design, or any other art form, music is complex and always changing. It would be slightly nutty to think that the Bible would address all the varying nuances and forms that music could take over centuries of human creativity. But, as with every other part of our lives, God's Word cuts right to the heart on the topic of music with clear principles that guide us no matter where culture decides to drift. While I may quote secular sources and studies in these pages, the final authority for these principles is the Word of God—and I intend to share many portions of Scripture for you to consider.

Fifth, this is a very broad topic to address in such a short book. We could easily fill volumes with information, instruction, and documentation about music. I confess right up front—these pages are not intended to be exhaustive, nor are they intended to address every question. You may finish this book and feel that so much was "left unsaid." I simply desire to share biblical principles and biblical reasons about the power of music in your heart—perhaps in a way that you've never considered.

Finally, you must understand the heart from which these words flow. Though I lead music in my church and I enjoy playing and writing music—it is not my god. These thoughts are not the overflow of a biased heart with an ax to grind. In reality, music is more of a hobby to me than a calling. It is merely one of many methods of communication that is a part of my spiritual growth and my ministry.

These chapters flow first from the heart of a Christian who has personally wrestled with the power of music and its influence upon his spirit. Yes, I confess that I have wrestled with this. God's work in my life regarding music has been a journey. It involved growing, sincerely seeking the heart of God, and being willing to enthrone Him in this area. Sometimes I failed. Sometimes I've had a wrong spirit. At times, as a younger man, I leaned toward the "I want my MTV" attitude of my generation—not really wanting to know what God thought. There were times I would have rather had Him step aside and accept what I wanted.

Gradually, over the years, God has gently reaffirmed through His Spirit and His Word, that my music has profound power and influence in my life. Understanding that power and considering that influence has caused me to make some very personal and very serious decisions about what I listen to, play, and write.

These chapters also flow from the heart of a youth pastor who is immersed daily in the struggles of young hearts and families. For nearly twenty years, I have become increasingly amazed at the common denominator of *music* in teenage struggles and its centrality to those struggles. I see plainly, every day of my life, what different kinds of music do to impressionable young hearts and to the family as a whole. I see what the personal choices of parents eventually produce in children. It's flat scary (and somewhat amazing) what music can do to a life and to a home.

Finally, these chapters flow from the heart of a father. The Lord has blessed Dana and me with three wonderful children. Their hearts are precious to us. For years we have attempted to protect their inner lives—to stand in the gap spiritually, and to make up the hedge. I refuse to give their hearts over to the power of music undiscerningly, and I refuse to selfishly allow my own "tastes" or "personal preferences" to become the breach through which Satan can attack them in the future.

After a couple of hours reading this book, you will set it down—either agreeing or disagreeing with what you've read. At least get the spirit. It's not argumentative, arrogant, or audacious. I'm not creating controversy. Let's both set aside our pride. I dare you to let down your defense for the next one hundred pages. What do you have to lose? Use discernment, but don't argue me as you read—rather, hear me out. More importantly—forget me and hear God out.

Ask His Holy Spirit to either confirm or deny what I will share with you—through His Word and in your heart. Then, when you set this book down, forget my opinions and just go with God. Whatever He says—do.

CHAPTER ONE

Music Matters
Understanding the Moral Significance of Music

If I walked over to a piano and played a note, could you tell me if that note is good or bad? Is it righteous or evil? Does that note intrinsically carry some moral value? Obviously not. Random notes are no different than random colors, random threads, or random letters. They carry no messages by themselves—they are but tools of communication.

What about the color red—is it good or bad? What about a piece of cloth or the letter "E"—are they good or bad? Do the raw ingredients of our multiple forms of communications and art carry moral value? No.

Doesn't that logically lead us to believe that music is amoral? Wouldn't it make sense to believe that music by itself, apart from words, carries no intrinsic moral influence? Well, let's consider.

MUSIC IN CONTEXT

It's all about context. Color has enormous emotional impact depending upon how it is applied. Individual letters form words with meaning when strung together by a messenger.

If you place random colors in the hands of a painter, that painter can use his brush to paint a picture. Does the combination of colors and brush strokes now have moral implications? Absolutely. Essentially, the painter has crafted a message—either for good or bad. His painting could be something beautiful or something vulgar.

If you place "amoral" letters at the finger tips of a writer, and that writer begins to type—the resulting message has power for either good or bad. While the letters by themselves are without moral significance, the moment they form a thought, they carry value for right or wrong.

Saying that music is "amoral" (without moral value) is true only in its intrinsic raw form—before human creativity comes into the picture. But all "earthly" music must be created by "earthly" beings. Raw notes are but the toolbox or the "color palette" from which the artist creates his message. Once the human touch has created the message, it's always either good or bad—always.

Just as art can be vulgar, clothing can be provocative, and words can be corrupt; even so music can communicate and facilitate messages that are wrong or harmful.

Here's the important question. Does the Bible teach this or is it just common sense? Actually—both. The Bible clearly supports the power of music being useful for good and bad. Some choose to ignore it; some perceive it as a threat; but the truth is there if we will allow it entrance into our hearts.

TROUBLE WITH AN EVIL SPIRIT

In 1 Samuel 16, we see a vivid picture of the moral qualities of music at work. In this chapter, King Saul is having significant spiritual struggles. He's dealing with anger, bitterness, envy, and rage toward God. The Lord was allowing this struggle (as He does so often in all of our lives) and patiently dealing with Saul.

Here's the biblical account: "But the Spirit of the LORD departed from Saul, and an evil spirit from the LORD troubled him. And Saul's servants said unto him, Behold now, an evil spirit from God troubleth thee. Let our lord now command thy servants, which are before thee, to seek out a man, who is a cunning player on an harp: and it shall come to pass, when the evil spirit from God is upon thee, that he shall play with his hand, and thou shalt be well" (1 Samuel 16:14–16).

God is clear that this was not merely a surface emotional struggle in Saul's life. It was a spiritual struggle in the heart, and music played a massive role in resolving it.

Here's the conclusion to the story: "And it came to pass, when the evil spirit from God was upon Saul, that David took an harp, and played with his hand: so Saul was refreshed, and was well, and the evil spirit departed from him" (1 Samuel 16:23).

What more solid biblical proof could we find for the moral value of music? God, in His own Word, shows us an "evil spirit"—a heart-level spiritual battle against the "principalities and powers" of Ephesians 6—literally chased away, scared off, "departed" when the right music was played. That's pretty powerful stuff!

TROUBLE WITH A GOLDEN CALF

Now, let's contrast this with another biblical illustration. Rewind the story back several hundred years to Exodus. The children of Israel have been released from bondage in Egypt and miraculously rescued and preserved by God. For many years they have been enslaved by a pagan nation with pagan rituals and corrupt practices of worship. Yet, God is calling them unto Himself. He desires that they separate from the paganism of their past and become fully His.

As the story unfolds, Moses has gone to Mount Sinai to be with God; Joshua is with him on the journey, and Aaron has been left back at camp to "hold down the fort." When Moses didn't return soon enough, the people of Israel became restless and began to pressure Aaron to fashion some new gods. Basically, they wanted to party in the paganism of their past rather than wait on the Lord. And that's exactly what they did.

They fashioned a golden calf, held a feast, and corrupted themselves before God. You must understand the godlessness of this moment. These people were engaging in pagan wickedness from a defiled past. This was far more than just an innocent feast, and God was very angry with this godless behavior.

Interestingly, in the middle of this pagan worship and idolatry we find *music*. "And when Joshua heard the noise of the people as they shouted, he said unto Moses, There is a noise of war in the camp. And he said, It is not the voice of them that shout for mastery, neither is it the voice of them that cry for being overcome: but the noise of them that sing do I hear" (Exodus 32:17–18).

Did you catch that? They were singing, but their singing sounded like "the noise of war"! Amazing. Why didn't the "evil spirits" of paganism flee this scene as they did in Saul's story? Why did David's harp playing facilitate the *departure* of evil, but the children of Israel's "war-like" music facilitated an *increase* in evil? If music is morally neutral, how could it have any impact for good or evil at all?

In one scenario, music facilitated pagan worship, in another it facilitated spiritual renewal. Was music the cause? No. Sin in the heart was the cause, but music was a direct contributor to the moral circumstances of both stories—a facilitator for both good and evil. In neither story is music "neutral." It is integrally a part of spiritual warfare in both passages.

WHEN GOD SHOWS UP

Here's one more illustration. Several hundred years after the golden calf, we find the children of Israel gathered once again to worship. This time, Solomon is king and he has now completed the construction of the temple. This has been God's work, and the people have labored, sacrificed, and honored the Lord in it.

When we come to 2 Chronicles 5, we are reading of the "grand opening" of the temple. In the first verses of the chapter we see God's people sacrificing and making their hearts right before Him. This is a sacred, holy time of worship. A few verses later we read:

> "Also the Levites which were the singers, all of them of Asaph, of Heman, of Jeduthun, with their sons and their brethren, being arrayed in white linen, having cymbals and psalteries and harps, stood at the east end of the altar, and with them an hundred and twenty priests sounding with trumpets:) It came even to pass, as the trumpeters and singers were as one, to make one sound to be heard in praising and thanking the LORD; and when they lifted up their voice with the trumpets and cymbals and instruments of musick, and praised the LORD, saying, For he is good; for his mercy endureth for ever: that then the house was filled with a cloud, even the house of the LORD; So that the priests could not stand to minister by reason of the cloud: for the glory of the LORD had filled the house of God."
> —2 Chronicles 5:12–14

In this case, when the music was played, it wasn't evil or evil spirits that showed up—but rather God Himself! But look closer—God says, "to make one sound to be heard in praising and thanking the LORD...." This music sounded like worship! Amazing!

In one passage music defeats evil spiritual powers, in another it sounds "war-like" and accompanies paganism, and in yet another, it invites the presence of God with the sound of "praise." Three distinct styles, three distinct sounds, and three distinct spiritual outcomes! That's powerful!

How can we as Christians ignore such clear evidence that different kinds of music send different kinds of messages—some good, some bad?

Three stories—one simple truth. Music communicates spiritually. Which means, music always has a spiritual (moral or immoral) message. It cannot be neutral or amoral unless it remains uncreated in its most basic and raw form (i.e. a single note).

Many popular Christian leaders today assert that "God created and likes all kinds of music." Friend, honestly, think about it. Does God like all forms of art since He created creativity? Does God approve of all forms of verbal and written expression since He created language? Obviously not. Never in Scripture does God place a universal stamp of approval upon all kinds and types of music. We'll see later that quite the opposite is true. The only way one can arrive at that conclusion is by starting with a presupposition and rationalizing backwards.

One final thought on the neutrality of music. In the history of humanity and Christendom, this has never been an argument until the 1960s with the development of Christian Contemporary Music (CCM). In fact, modern Christianity is the *only* group on the planet that even espouses that music is "amoral." Nobody but CCM Christians actually believe this. Sadly, more and more Christians in every generation are buying into this lie.

WHAT THE WORLD KNOWS

May I share with you what even *unregenerate* people have to say about music and its moral or spiritual power? Here are just a few quotes:

Pietro Mascagni, Italian Composer (1863–1945) said, "*Modern music is as dangerous as narcotics.*"

Aristotle said, "*Music has a power of forming the character, and should therefore be introduced into the education of the young.*"

Plato taught, "*In order to take the spiritual temperature of an individual or a society, one must mark the music.*"

Paul Kantner of the "Jefferson Airplane" said, "*The new rock music is intended to broaden the generation gap, alienate parents from their children, and prepare young people for revolution.*"

Dr. Howard Hanson, an authority on music, stated in *The American Journal of Psychiatry*: "*Music is a curiously subtle art with innumerable, varying emotional connotations. It is made up of many ingredients and according to the proportions of those components, it can be soothing or invigorating, ennobling or vulgarizing…. It has powers for evil as well as for good."*

Henry David Thoreau said, *"Music…has helped cause the destruction of the Greek and Roman empires and it will sooner or later destroy America and England."*

Cheetah (magazine) quoted a musician as saying, *"If the establishment knew what today's popular music is saying, not what the words are saying, but what the music itself is saying, they would just turn their thumb down on it. They'd ban it. They'd smash all the records and arrest anyone who tried to play it."*

The late Neil Postman stated in his book, *Amusing Ourselves to Death*: *"To maintain that technology [music] is neutral…is…stupidity plain and simple."*

Dr. Max Schoen wrote in *The Psychology of Music*: *"The medical, psychiatric and other evidence for the non-neutrality of music is so overwhelming that it frankly amazes me that anyone should seriously say otherwise."*

Frank Zappa said, *"The loud sounds and bright lights are tremendous indoctrination tools; it is possible to modify the human chemical structure with the right combination of* frequencies. If the right kind of beat makes you tap your foot, what kind of beat makes you curl your fist and strike?"

Christian author, Tim Fisher wrote in *The Battle for Christian Music*: "*It is almost impossible to overstate the absurdity of the claim that music is neutral, amoral, or void of communication by itself…. Those who have looked beyond the current music publications know that no one has ever taken the position that music is neutral except for Christians in the last twenty-five years….*"

Finally, in his book, *The Marketing of Evil*, David Kupelian uses this quote from a communications professor at NYU to expose the moral decay of today's "rock music society", "*It's part of the official rock video world view… that your parents are creeps, teachers are nerds and idiots, authority figures are laughable, nobody can really understand kids except the corporate sponsor.*"

Have you ever considered that every Hollywood composer intimately knows and understands the communicative power of music? They know what tones, what instruments, and what harmonies to use to make you feel scared, sad, happy, silly, or nostalgic! They are masters at communicating with music alone.

As a Christian, I urge you to care about the spiritual power that music has in your life. Rather than presume unfoundedly that music is "amoral"—take heed to the admonition of God when He says, "See then that ye walk circumspectly, not as fools, but as wise…Wherefore be ye not unwise, but understanding what the will of the Lord is. …be filled with the Spirit; Speaking to yourselves in psalms and hymns and spiritual songs, singing and making melody in your heart to the Lord" (Ephesians 5:15, 17–19).

In this passage God warns us to be *wise* and to walk *circumspectly* (looking in every direction). We're to be looking for and seeing dangers that the rest of the world just won't see. Let us not be blinded by our personal tastes. Let us not be threatened by God's truth—as though He is about to steal our favorite CDs and rob us of our favorite forms of entertainment.

The truth that music has moral value is a blessing! It's a wonderful gift. We'll see more of this later, so stay with me!

Even lost men believe in the moral value of music, but they don't have the conscience to care. For the most part, dead hearts don't care about spiritual messages—it's all about entertainment. May we have a heart to care and a conscience to sense the obvious truth.

Think about what we've learned—David's "harp" music scared off an evil spirit; Israel's "war-like" music facilitated pagan idolatry. Solomon's "sound to be heard in praising" allowed God to show up personally!

Music never has been and never will be morally neutral because it always carries a message from the heart of the messenger. Music's message is intimately related to our emotional and spiritual lives—always. But this is just the beginning—let's press on.

CHAPTER TWO

American Idol
Bowing to Culture's Entertainment god

Over the past few generations, America has developed a passionate infatuation with a new idol—*entertainment.* Have you considered lately how much of our lives fit into the entertainment category and how obsessed our culture is with being entertained?

ENTERTAINMENT—IT'S EVERYWHERE

From movies, to music, to television shows, to computers, to video games, to cell phones, to iPods and beyond— we *must* be entertained! We are a culture so driven by entertainment that it must be with us at all times—on demand, at our fingertips at any instant!

Recently, I was eating dinner with a friend at a restaurant here in Southern California called "The ESPN

Zone." Taking sports and entertainment to new heights, this restaurant literally has TV monitors wall to wall and even in the restroom stalls!

Even our modern news entertains us. From wars, to train wrecks, to political discourse, to suicide bombers, to sports playoffs—it's all creatively presented with energetic music, flashy motion graphics, attractive anchors, and creatively worded scripts. We make movies out of national tragedies, global leaders out of entertainers, cults out of music groups, and one-hour specials out of major disasters.

We are addicted to being entertained. We are a culture of broken relationships, empty lives, hurting homes, and brainless forward momentum—mindlessly being moved through time while amused and distracted by the noise and motion of media. It is the equivalent of putting our intellect in neutral while our hearts are manipulated.

Why not? After all, it *does* make us feel better. When life is painful, we can create a new one online. When life is stressful, we can vegetate in front of the TV. When life is quiet, we can put in our earbuds. Entertainment is where we turn to escape reality. It is a painkiller for our souls and Novocaine for our hearts. It's where we take our empty lives to create the illusion of satisfaction and significance. When reality is pointless, purposeless, and painful—there's always fantasy playing on some screen or iPod nearby.

I'm not saying that every technology or every medium is evil, nor am I saying that it is wrong to enjoy entertainment—with spiritually healthy influences and in balance. Our culture, however, has taken entertainment to its extreme. We live for it; we give colossal amounts of time to it, and we allow it to dictate many of our life values. It dominates us. When we're at work, we talk about it. When we drive, we listen to it. When we're at home, we watch it. When we're sleeping, we dream about it. And when we just need a break and take a vacation, we immerse in it! Entertainment is truly the American idol!

MUSIC AS ENTERTAINMENT?

Somewhere along the way, Christians began to believe that music is for *entertainment*—that it is primarily for our enjoyment. We adapted to the idolatry of culture and began to view our music as a vehicle for our pleasure. This new belief has led to an entirely new approach to music in church and in the Christian life over the past fifty years—a new philosophy of entertainment-based worship. Gradually, Christian music became "all about us" and our style preferences—what makes us feel good. As a result, worship became more about us than God and our excuse is, "God likes all kinds of music."

Amazingly, fifty years later, this entertainment approach to music and worship has given way to a new kind of church altogether—one that more closely resembles the combination of a late-night talk show and a pop concert. These are churches where the radical, spiritual transformation that Christ brings to a life has all but come to a grinding halt as we've set aside the true God to bow to the entertainment god! Nobody leaves church changed, but everybody liked the music, so they'll be back next Sunday to feel good again.

Allow me to cut right to the point. One would find it impossible to make any biblical case that music should hold such an idolatrous place in our lives and churches. The Bible does not portray music as *primarily* for entertainment. It does not teach us that music is to be self-serving or self-glorifying. That is not to say that God's people cannot *enjoy* music or find pleasure in it, but simply that this is not God's *primary* purpose for music.

BOWING TO THE WRONG GOD

Culture's idolatrous addiction to music is a reflection of paganism, not godliness. And when we enthrone our musical tastes and view them as vital entertainment, we too reflect a pagan mindset. Much like culture's increasing perversion and preoccupation with sex, music in culture has become a reflection of a world pursuing pleasure. I'm afraid that music for many Christians and churches has become the same.

As Christians, music does not deserve the throne of our hearts. I've met many Christians who literally choose a church by its musical styles rather than its biblical beliefs. Personally, in wrestling with this subject I've been tempted to cling to my musical tastes and style preferences as though they were essential to my personal happiness. I've known many who wouldn't dare read a book like this with an open heart simply because of the threat that it posed to their private entertainment.

This mindset is nothing less than idolatry. It was wrong in my heart, and it's wrong in the heart of any Christian. And until recently, Christianity did not look at music this way. Music in the Bible never held this kind of place in the hearts of God's people. Only the Word of God and the Lord Jesus Christ had this kind of preeminence in first century Christianity.

Music is not primarily for our pleasure. This thought pattern reflects the world's teaching, not God's. In actuality, *we* are created for *God's* pleasure! It's all about Him. It's not about "what we desire" but "what He desires." It's not about our tastes, but rather His commands. It's not about our preferences, but rather His precepts.

We have so lost God's original intent in the mass media generation. We have so elevated our personal pleasure and entertainment in our music, that personal desire overrules all other biblical thinking. We stop our ears and close our hearts to any consideration that a particular musical style may be harmful or spiritually dangerous, especially if it happens to be a style that we "like." Our personal tastes have become the standard by which we discern the acceptability and spiritual value of all music. In other words, "If I like it, it must be okay! If I like it, then surely God likes it!"

Why do we think this way about music, yet we would flinch at thinking this way in any other part of our Christian life? The Bible doesn't teach an "if it feels good do it" or "if it feels good, God must like it" mentality. We don't teach our children that God likes all kinds of words, all kinds of thoughts, or all kinds of sexual activity! Why is "our" music immune and exempt from biblical examination and reason?

For many, musical preferences have become what the Bible calls a "strong hold"—literally a faulty thinking pattern based on lies and deception. Second Corinthians 10:4 says, "For the weapons of our warfare are not carnal, but mighty through God to the pulling down of strong holds."

IT'S ONLY SOUND

Let me ask you an honest question. Is your music subject to God's approval? If you discovered that He desired for you to listen to a different kind of music, would you obey willingly and gladly? Or would you resist and cling to "what you like"?

Recently in a counseling session, I was speaking with a teenage young man about the power of music. After some thought about how strongly his music was holding on to his heart, he lifted his head, sort of chuckled and said, "It's kind of strange when you really think about it...it's only music...it's only sound."

Oh, but how powerful that sound is! Just try to take away or suggest danger in the favorite CD or the favorite CCM group of a supposedly "surrendered" Christian. You'll get everything from rage to ridicule—real fruits of the Spirit—all qualities that are produced by just such "good, godly music." I'm being intentionally sarcastic to cause you to think. If pop-styled Christian music is so spiritually effective, why aren't we having revival? Why isn't it producing more holy, more separated, more godly individuals? Why are young people leaving Christianity in record numbers? Why do we *have to have* the world's music?

Should music really be such a stronghold in the Christian heart or in the local church? Should such self-absorption be the guiding force of our choices in entertainment? Should we view our music as entertainment at all? Does God really like "all kinds" of music?

Music has a much higher purpose than our pleasure. Reducing music to mere entertainment would be something like asking a brain surgeon to roast marshmallows for a living. No, music is much too powerful and spiritually significant to reduce it to a petty place of pleasure.

First Corinthians 10:14 admonishes us, "Wherefore, my dearly beloved, flee from idolatry." Again in Colossians 3:5 we're told to, "Mortify therefore your members which are upon the earth; fornication, uncleanness, inordinate affection, evil concupiscence, and covetousness, which is idolatry."

God commands us to "mortify" or "put to death" our "members." Anything less than full surrender of our bodies (including our ears) to God is a subtle form of idolatry.

Is music an idol in your life? Is it a stronghold? Are you addicted to *your* style, *your* group, *your* sound? Do you find yourself putting up a wall of defense in your heart, even as you read these words? Is your primary concern that it "makes you feel good" or that you listen to "what you like"?

Think about it. It's only sound.

IT'S WHAT I LIKE

Recently, a non-Christian who visited our church said something interesting to me. He referenced that he enjoyed our music and that he was delighted to hear something different than the rest of the world. He said, "It was actually 'Christian music.'" Then he proceeded to say, "That idea of Christian rock? That's ridiculous...if it's rock, it's not Christian, and if it's Christian, it's not rock."

If lost men can tell the difference between good music and bad, why can't Christians? God says that in the last days, men would be "traitors, heady, highminded, lovers of pleasures more than lovers of God" (2 Timothy 3:4). When we love our music more than we love God, we've strayed far off course. When we're so self-centered in our thinking that lost men are clearly seeing what we deny, something must change.

Contrast this with an interesting note. Recently a large "seeker-sensitive" style church with multiple weekend services decided to begin a new service—one with hymns and less contemporary music for those who prefer a "more conservative worship style." They chose to call that service

"The Divine Hour." Hmmm, what does that say about all the other hours? It seems that even CCM Christianity intuitively knows the difference between the "divine" and the defiled.

This idolatry of music in our hearts leads us to two basic conclusions that are false. The first is, "I must listen to what I like." Our fleshly appetites become the first test of whether music is "good" or not. Where do we find this principle in the Bible? We don't. We find it from a heart that has a greatly inflated sense of pleasure. God never instructs us to allow our appetites to rule our lives. Rather, He instructs us to bring our bodies into subjection, to allow the Holy Spirit to fill us, and to let His peace rule in our hearts. He teaches us to deny ungodliness, even though it may be appealing.

The second erroneous conclusion is, "I must worship with what I like." The whole CCM movement flows from an effort to make church what men like. And along the way, we have instructed a generation that worship is more about selfish appetites than it is about the holiness of God. We live in a day when people choose churches based upon the entertainment value rather than the biblical doctrine. Our mentality is, "If I don't like the music, then I can't worship there!"

THE ENTERTAINMENT GOD

Welcome to the entertainment age—where mankind is ever thirsting, panting, longing after amusement with an insatiable desire to be pleased; where humanity is heedless of the heart effects of entertainment; and where even "worship" is self serving because it makes us "feel good."

Sadly, it is possible to feel good while you're dying. And while the world is dying without Christ, Christianity is greatly diminishing for neglect of His basic precepts.

CCM style churches are losing a vast majority (some estimate 96%) of their young people after high school graduation. We've rocked them well, but we've taught them to worship the wrong god. Entertainment-style Christianity is not noticeably different in any way from the rest of the world—and why would it be if we're bowing to the same idol? Why should our young people stay faithful to Christ, or why should an unsaved man desire Christ at all when entertainment is god—both in and out of church?

Many Christians live for their music. It possesses them. Friend, God never intended for your personal desires and tastes to be so powerful in your life—in any area.

American idol? That's a great name for it—for that is truly what it is. We might expect it from the world, but Christians should know better.

"Little children, keep yourselves from idols. Amen."
—1 John 5:21

CHAPTER THREE

The Soundtrack of Our Lives
Understanding Music's Power in Culture

We've seen in chapter one that music is not neutral, but rather very powerful for both good and evil. Chapter two exposed a culture that has elevated music and entertainment to a place of over-blown priority—idolatry. But what does all this mean and what is the spiritual nature of it all, behind the scenes?

Over twenty years ago, Alan Bloom wrote in a best-selling book, *The Closing of the American Mind*, "Nothing is more singular about this generation than its addiction to music. This is the age of music and the states of soul that accompany it. ...It is their passion; nothing else excites them as it does; they cannot take seriously anything alien to music." He continues, "Music...provides an unquestionable justification and a fulfilling pleasure to the activities it accompanies.... Armed with music, man can [disregard] rational doubt. Out of music emerges the gods that suit it, and they educate men by their example and their commandments."

He goes on to say, "Rock music has one appeal only, a barbaric appeal, to sexual desire—not love…but sexual desire undeveloped and untutored. …Rock music gives children on a silver platter, with all the public authority of the entertainment industry, everything their parents used to teach them to wait for."

Music is not only an idol in today's culture, it is an addiction, and it is the primary tool that Satan uses to indoctrinate, control, and manipulate the hearts and minds of the masses. Before we see this in Scripture, I want to tell you the story of a very important company in your life.

MUSIC OR MUZAK?

Ever heard of Muzak? Whether or not you've heard *of* Muzak, I assure you, you have heard Muzak! Muzak is the company that pioneered the idea that music can accompany everyday life. This company began in the 1940s by providing background music for various settings like elevators, doctors' offices, etc. (Remember, this was before the average American could carry music with them at all times.) And over the decades, perhaps no group on the planet has studied the power of music more than the researchers at Muzak.

An article from *The New Yorker* magazine in April of 2006 quotes, "…Today, [Muzak] estimates that its daily audience is roughly a hundred million people, in more than a dozen countries, and that it supplies 60% of the commercial background music in the United States."

Muzak offers a service known as "audio architecture" to more than 350 corporations around the globe. Audio architecture is essentially the power of public influence and control—through music. Their clients include major restaurant chains such as "Outback Steakhouse" as well as a host of retail chains like "Old Navy." Chances are, if you've been anywhere in public in recent days, you've been subjected to Muzak's influence without even knowing it. This is a company that owes its success to the manipulative power of music in mass culture. Muzak simply could not exist if music did not affect the attitudes and behavior of people.

The New Yorker article tells this story, "In the forties, Muzak introduced a trademarked concept, called Stimulus Progression, which held that most workers would be more productive if they were exposed to music of gradually increasing intensity, in fifteen minute cycles. The process was said to be subliminal: Muzak affected you the way hypnosis did, whether you wanted it to or not. Only sanitized instrumental arrangements were used, because the absence of lyrics made the music less likely to intrude upon conscious thought. It was sometimes said that if the songs in a Stimulus Progression program were played in reverse order, a listener would helplessly fall asleep."

Think about that. Music affects us *subliminally*—often in a way that does not intrude upon our *"conscious thought."*

The article continues, "…the first thing many of us do when we find ourselves alone with our thoughts is to reach for the handiest means of drowning them out—by putting on a pair of headphones, or by sliding a disk into the car's CD player. Audio architecture is a compelling concept because the human response to musical accompaniment is powerful and involuntary. 'Our biggest competitor,' a member of Muzak's marketing department told me, 'is silence.'"

Did you catch that? "The human response to musical accompaniment is *powerful* and *involuntary*…." Are you getting the message? Are you understanding how powerful and dominant music is in our culture?

Look at Muzak's own promotional words and consider them from a biblical viewpoint. "Audio Architecture is *emotion* by *design*. Our innovation and our inspiration, it is the integration of music, voice and sound to create experiences that link customers with companies. Its power lies in its *subtlety*. It bypasses the *resistance* of the mind and targets the *receptiveness* of the heart. When people are made to feel good in, say, a store, they feel good about that store. They like it. Remember it. Go back to it. Audio Architecture builds a bridge to loyalty. And loyalty is what keeps brands alive." (Quote From Muzak website, November 2006)

Researchers at this company literally tell us that music is "*emotion by design*" and that it "bypasses the *resistance* of the *mind* and targets the *receptiveness* of the *heart*."

Muzak makes millions of dollars annually by creating public soundtracks for our daily lives—soundtracks for retail stores, restaurants, malls, and dozens of other public places. These soundtracks bypass our intellectual resistance and create involuntary, heart-level emotions and responses! That is powerful!

Consider this. If Muzak can do this with music, what can *Satan* do with music? More importantly what *is* Satan doing with music and what is the music of culture doing to my heart?

If music is this powerful and important for mass marketing, how powerful is it in the spiritual realm and in our relationship to Christ?

SEDUCING SPIRITS

Before we get lost in the endless research of secular culture, let's consider what the Bible says about this matter. Let's take a look at some guiding principles and see if we can connect the dots.

> "Beloved, believe not every spirit, but try the spirits whether they are of God: because many false prophets are gone out into the world. Hereby know ye the Spirit of God: Every spirit that confesseth that Jesus Christ is come in the flesh is of God: And every spirit

that confesseth not that Jesus Christ is come in the flesh is not of God: and this is that spirit of antichrist, whereof ye have heard that it should come; and even now already is it in the world. Ye are of God, little children, and have overcome them: because greater is he that is in you, than he that is in the world. They are of the world: therefore speak they of the world, and the world heareth them. We are of God: he that knoweth God heareth us; he that is not of God heareth not us. Hereby know we the spirit of truth, and the spirit of error."—1 John 4:1–6

This passage talks about two voices in the world today—the Spirit of God and spirit of antichrist. In these verses God challenges us to "try the spirits"—in other words to discern what is impacting our hearts, our emotions, our spiritual beings—to consider what voices we are "hearing," whether they are of God or not. God says that this "spirit of antichrist" is in the world, but that we have "overcome" them because God *in us* is greater than this "spirit."

Don't miss this! Verses 5 and 6 then say, "They are of the world: therefore speak they of the world, and the world heareth them. We are of God: he that knoweth God heareth us; he that is not of God heareth not us...." In other words, these evil spirits are not only *in* the world, but they are *speaking* and being *heard*. These are satanic, spiritual beings using some physical means to speak to the world and to be heard. They are speaking specifically "of the world" and they have the ears of the masses. Interesting.

What a contrast God brings forth when He says, "We are of God: he that knoweth God heareth us...." In other words, Christians give their ears, hence their hearts, to a different Voice than the world! Those that are of God listen to a different Spirit! They discern the difference and the danger, and they lend their ears to different influences than the rest of the world!

Now, before you rule this passage out as having nothing to do with music, think again. Obviously, the voices of false spirits would not be limited to music alone, but dare we think that music is not a major part of how Satan's principalities and powers are speaking in today's culture?

Let me ask you some questions. Amongst all the forms of entertainment media, what is the most pervasive? What is the loudest most inescapable voice of all forms of communication? What is everywhere all the time? What "bypasses the resistance of the mind and targets the receptiveness of the heart"? Music. What communicates subliminally? What is "emotion by design"? What permeates every form of media on the planet today? Music. Can you think of any *voice* that "the world" is giving an ear to more than music?

Don't misunderstand. I'm not saying that all music is dangerous or evil. I'm saying that there are dangerous forms of music as well as healthy forms—and one brief study of mass culture proves that the world's music is dangerous, whether it has "Christian words" or not.

THE BATTLE FOR CONTROL

Proverbs 4:23 states, "Keep thy heart with all diligence; for out of it are the issues of life." You see, Satan wants control of your spirit—your heart. Out of your heart flows every other issue of your life! If he gains that ground, all other ground can eventually become his. He wants victory *inside* you first!

He wants to dethrone the Holy Spirit of God and he desires to dictate every emotion, every thought, and eventually every action and decision! He does not want you to be filled with the Holy Spirit and speaking to yourself with "psalms and hymns and spiritual songs." "And be not drunk with wine, wherein is excess; but be filled with the Spirit; Speaking to yourselves in psalms and hymns and spiritual songs, singing and making melody in your heart to the Lord" (Ephesians 5:18–19).

He wants to control your heart and mind, to subvert truth through your imagination, and to take your life away from strong spiritual influences. And no tool in his arsenal is so powerful, so seductive, and so subtle as *music*. In contrast, God teaches us this principle: "Casting down imaginations, and every high thing that exalteth itself against the knowledge of God, and bringing into captivity every thought to the obedience of Christ" (2 Corinthians 10:5).

I submit to you that music is the most prominent, powerful, and pervasive form of communication that satanic spirits are using today to control and shape our mass culture. Everywhere you turn, the world is hearing. Everywhere you listen, these voices are speaking. And everywhere you look, music is shaping the emotions, the spirit, and the hearts of people.

Nearly twenty-five years ago, while the rise of modern pop music was still gaining momentum, *Family Weekly* magazine reported in 1983, "Music is used everywhere to condition the human mind. It can be just as powerful as a drug and much more dangerous, because nobody takes musical manipulation very seriously." And in 1940 (about the same time Muzak was discovering music's power) Dr. Max Schoen wrote in *The Psychology of Music*, "Music is the most powerful stimulus known among the perceptive senses…."

To an unbelieving culture, this information would be meaningless. But for the Christian, may God enlighten the eyes of our understanding ("The eyes of your understanding being enlightened…" —Ephesians 1:18) so that we may see the godless trance that music has placed upon our culture as a whole. May we see the spiritual control and may we understand the battle for the hearts of men that is really going on behind the scenes!

This battle is real. This battle is of global proportions. Yes, music in culture is very powerful, but far more importantly, this battle is personal.

Let's find out why.

"Now the Spirit speaketh expressly, that in the latter times some shall depart from the faith, giving heed to seducing spirits, and doctrines of devils;" —1 Timothy 4:1

"For all that is in the world, the lust of the flesh, and the lust of the eyes, and the pride of life, is not of the Father, but is of the world."—1 John 2:16

CHAPTER FOUR

The Soundtrack of Our Hearts
Understanding Music's Power in My Personal Life

One of my earliest childhood memories is that of my father practicing with his band in the basement of our home near Baltimore, Maryland. From that day until this, I have unavoidably been immersed in the music industry—and not always for the good!

A UNIQUE PERSPECTIVE

The first few years of my life, my father played and sang pop music in local bands. He had been drawn away from Christ in the early sixties by music that most "Christians" would consider harmless today. In truth it was anything but harmless. Had it continued to maintain a stronghold in my family, my life would have turned out quite differently! Thankfully, the Spirit of God wasn't done speaking in my father's heart, and by the time I was reaching my fifth birthday, he and my mother (unsaved at the time) were both seeing the negative impacts of their own popular music and culture upon me and my two younger brothers. Looking back on our journey, it is obvious that my dad's decision to step away from his music addiction was a pivotal first step in God's sovereign plan for bringing my family back to Him. Somewhere in the core of his being, he knew this music was hurting our home. I'm thankful that he listened to God's voice over his own desires.

Throughout the rest of my childhood and young adult years, my father was involved "behind the scenes" in the music industry in various sales positions for pro-audio equipment and instruments. At the same time, through God's marvelous grace, we were saved and began to grow as committed Christians in a conservative, Bible-believing church with a wonderful, Christ-like music ministry. This experience allowed a stark contrast to present itself in my life. The difference between the world's music and God's music became very clear and basic to me, even at a young age.

This all gave me a very unique perspective on the power of music and the secular music industry. God allowed me to see and experience the wholesome, biblical product in my own heart and home of *godly* music, while simultaneously allowing me many contrasting experiences where I could, from a safe distance, see the twisted, wicked, godless, and perverted lifestyles of those immersed in the world's music. This wasn't an MTV or a CD sales-rack view, but rather a behind the scenes look at the realities of the secular music industry. Though I was in my elementary years, the difference between what is godly and what is pagan was blatantly clear. The product of both was plain to see.

I share this for two reasons. First, to say that my young Christian parents first saw the personal impact of music in our home when I was very young. Second, to say that God allowed me to clearly see, throughout my life, that music always facilitates and produces a lifestyle—it always powerfully dictates a personal response that is reflective of the nature of the music.

Music always produces a lifestyle.

More importantly, music influences *your* lifestyle!

Can I prove it biblically? Yes, in a moment. But first, consider this.

MUSIC PRODUCES A LIFESTYLE

If biblical examples, secular studies, Muzak, Hollywood, and common sense were all collectively wrong—meaning that music (regardless of the lyrics) was not directly influential upon the lifestyle of a person—why would Satan so aggressively use it in our world today? If music doesn't dictate heart attitudes and outward responses, then why are the most angry people on the planet addicted to angry music? Why are defiant people—including Christians—so immersed in music that promotes rebellion—by its very structural qualities and rhythmic patterns?

If musical styles don't have powerful messages, then why aren't contemporary Christian artists less like the world and more like Christ? Why are values like holiness, modesty, submission, and honor disappearing from contemporary churches? Why are the fruits of the Spirit— love, joy, peace, gentleness, and meekness—so hard to find in entertainment-driven, pseudo-Christian environments?

Why does the CCM movement walk so closely in step with the world's music, the world's artists, and the world's styles? This fact alone so clearly defies God's principle in Romans 12:2, "And be not conformed to this world: but be ye transformed by the renewing of your mind…." Why can we no longer tell a difference between what is Christian and what is not? And why do unsaved men look at Christianity as a poor, second-hand copy of what they already have— bondage to the short-term pleasures of sin?

It doesn't take a rocket scientist to simply look at culture and Christianity as a whole and conclude that, YES, *our music changes us!*

In the world, over the last sixty years, music has led us step by step away from morality and into hedonism. In the church, music has followed one step behind the world for two generations in spite of God's command to "Love not the world, neither the things that are in the world…" (1 John 2:15). Look where our disobedience has brought us. Ninety-six percent of CCM churched young people are walking away from God after high school graduation! Music has changed the world. Music has changed the church. Music has changed Christianity.

And music will change *you* too.

MUSIC CHANGES US

There's no arguing the point. Different styles of music create different emotions, different spirits, and thus, different lifestyles. For example, rap music and that which is beat driven to the extreme, produces extremely fleshly and even angry or violent lifestyles. The musical style you choose is reflected in your heart and your heart is reflected in your style—so much so that it becomes hard to distinguish which is the cause and which is the effect! Sensual music enlarges sensual desires, promotes sensual decisions, and leads to sensual lifestyles. The spark of the flesh combined with the fuel of music creates a raging fire that devours our hearts from the inside out.

Think it through yourself. Look at a style of music, then look at the lives of those who immerse in that style. The two go hand in hand—always.

In the mid 1900s, songwriter E. Y. Harburg wrote, "Words make you think a thought. Music makes you feel a feeling. A song makes you feel a thought." We already saw in the last chapter that music creates powerful emotions that in turn create a powerful and involuntary response. We saw that music bypasses our conscious thoughts and penetrates directly to the receptiveness of our hearts.

Yes, music changes you—either for good or bad. Unfortunately, we're losing the battle to seducing spirits in both secular culture as well as in the church. It's time we wise up to God's truth.

GOD'S MUSIC, GOD'S CHANGE

What does God have to say about this? Does He give indication in His Word that music (regardless of the words) produces a spiritual change within us?

In Ephesians 5:18–20, God commands us, "And be not drunk with wine, wherein is excess; but be filled with the Spirit; Speaking to yourselves in psalms and hymns and spiritual songs, singing and making melody in your heart to the Lord; Giving thanks always for all things unto God and the Father in the name of our Lord Jesus Christ."

In contrast to the passage in 1 John regarding wicked spirits speaking to the world, in this passage we're commanded to let God's Spirit have control. Remember the context—God is referencing the *spiritual battle* for our hearts. He desires control of our inner lives—our spirit and emotions. Notice directly after the command to be "filled with the Spirit" God brings *music* into the picture!

God connects our daily lifestyle, which is to be Spirit-led and controlled, directly to our musical habits! Amazing. In other words, He doesn't want Muzak determining your spiritual condition or dictating your emotions—He wants His Holy Spirit to have that place in your life!

He presents music as a key element to the battle for control. He brings music into the spiritual realm as a tool of spiritual transformation and growth. And He clearly states what "kind" or "style" of music that He intends for us to allow. He says, "psalms, hymns, and spiritual songs"— songs that we can both sing and make melody in our hearts to the Lord.

If we stopped right here, we could discount most CCM and secular pop music with this one verse, for the vast majority of this kind of music is heavily beat-driven (not melody, as the verse states) and certainly speaks more to the flesh than the spirit—in direct contradiction to God's command. He doesn't command us to be "filled with the flesh." He commands us to bring our bodies and our minds "into subjection" and "to the obedience of Christ." First Corinthians 9:27 says, "But I keep under my body, and bring it into subjection..." and again in 2 Corinthians 10:5 we're commanded "...and bringing into captivity every thought to the obedience of Christ."

It would take serious rationalization to reason that musical "style" isn't involved in Ephesians 5:19. One would have to literally choose to avoid the obvious—or choose to rewrite Scripture—one of the two. God makes it abundantly clear that certain "styles" of music will facilitate a Spirit-led lifestyle. He uses words to describe those styles—psalms, hymns, and spiritual songs—and songs with melody that flow from the heart.

YOU ARE WHAT YOU HEAR

Again, God directly connects my spiritual growth with my listening choices—"Let the word of Christ dwell in you richly in all wisdom; teaching and admonishing one another in psalms and hymns and spiritual songs, singing with grace in your hearts to the Lord" (Colossians 3:16).

What exactly is "singing with *grace*"? I would submit that it sounds vastly different from what we hear in the pop and CCM culture today—unless you believe that pop-culture suddenly has a grasp of God's amazing grace. I would suggest that "singing with grace" doesn't sound like "the noise of war in the camp."

What exactly is a "spiritual song"? Surely it would be the opposite of a "fleshly song." So which is it today? Which styles of music are fleshly and which are spiritual? If the world's music is suddenly "spiritual" then Christians have been wrong for thousands of years—going all the way back to the book of Acts. If the world's music is fleshly, then Christians have made a drastic mistake by following its styles so closely.

Speaking of the book of Acts, let's consider what style of music God prefers. I believe we've already answered this, but let me share another story from a time when the church used to be different from the world.

> "And at midnight Paul and Silas prayed, and sang praises unto God: and the prisoners heard them. And suddenly there was a great earthquake, so that

the foundations of the prison were shaken: and immediately all the doors were opened, and every one's bands were loosed."—Acts 16:25–26

What style of music were Paul and Silas singing in this jail? We know this—it wasn't CCM or pop (that's only been around for less than a century); it was understandable, and it pleased God enough for Him to manifest His presence in a special way! You see, when God is pleased with our praise, He inhabits our praise (Psalm 22:3). When He isn't pleased, He is grieved—as in Israel's dance around the golden calf. Could this be partially why CCM churches are seeing swelling, carnal crowds rather than real, spiritual revival and heart renewal? Have we gathered around culture's golden calf in the name of God? According to God's Word, I believe we have.

Consider the Scriptures we've seen—from Saul's trouble with an evil spirit, to Israel's pagan, war-like music, to Solomon's music that sounded like "praising," to God's warning about seducing spirits speaking in the world, to His instruction that spiritual music can facilitate a life controlled by His Holy Spirit! God truly presents a clear-cut case that our music as Christians has a profound personal impact upon our lives. He also makes it clear that He prefers a spiritual style of music.

Let me be very plain. As Muzak has proven that various kinds of music provokes various kinds of responses in us, God instructs that our music, as Christians, should provoke spiritual growth through His Holy Spirit. The world has musical styles that feed the flesh, and God teaches us of styles that promote godliness. Which will you choose to hear?

MUSIC IMPACTS MY INNER LIFE

Your music is intimately related to your spiritual battle. The choices you make when you turn on a CD or an iPod are intricately related to your inner life. You will either be led by the flesh or led by the Spirit of God. Your music is *changing* you. It is dictating emotions and heart responses that are either godly or ungodly. Those emotions are the product of either God's Holy Spirit growing you through godly music or your flesh capitalizing on the voices of seducing spirits!

Ultimately, your spiritual and emotional condition, as influenced by your music, will come out in your lifestyle. Your words, your deeds, your decisions, and your actions— the issues of your life— will all be a product of your heart and what you've placed into it. Your music directly affects your heart—both God and Muzak agree on that one.

Music creates emotion. Music creates context to life. Therefore, you ultimately think, feel, and act in response to what you hear. If you participate in the kind of music that Paul and Silas, Solomon's singers, and the psalmists created, then you can expect God to show up at work in your heart and life. If you hear the kind of music that Israel had before the golden calf, or that culture so clearly uses to live in the flesh, then you can expect to wrestle more than necessary with ungodliness in your life. It's just that simple.

We see these principles in Scripture and we see them clearly in culture and science. But allow me a moment to share something personally with you.

A PERSONAL STRUGGLE

Throughout my faith journey, there have been seasons when Satan wanted my music. In retrospect, the spiritual battle is as clear as day, though at the time it wasn't. I believe every Christian young person deals with this personal battle. Let's face it. Our flesh really likes the world's styles of music.

My first surrender in the area of music was not of my own will. It was when I was eight years old and my parents became youth workers at our church. In so doing, they made a commitment that we would not listen to the world's music. Quite honestly, even at eight years old, I thought this was ridiculous, and I even said so. I thought my parents were becoming unnecessarily "fanatical." In actuality, Satan was fighting to maintain control of my heart.

During the following years, Christ-honoring music became the dominant musical influence in our home, and believe it or not, God's Holy Spirit eventually won my heart. I discovered a spiritual thirst and heart-level appreciation for godly music.

But the battle returned years later. This time the surface battle was more over Christian contemporary music, but the heart issue was the same—Satan wanted influence over my spirit and emotions. I'm ashamed to admit it, but if there is an argument for the use of CCM and pop styles of music, I probably used it to rationalize my thinking over the years. Though I generally kept a "safe distance" from dangerous music in my own listening habits and I never fully immersed in a wrong style, I still battled in my heart over the validity of the reasoning presented in this book. I wondered if the world's music dressed in Christian lyrics and labels really was "all that harmful."

WHEN GOD WON

But there came a moment in my heart when the Holy Spirit of God penetrated my argumentative self-will and simply impressed this question—"Do you see any correlation between your spiritual battles and your music struggle?"

I must admit, this was a painful, convicting moment. The answer was a clear "yes." A second question followed, something like this—"Do you think your musical struggle is more about self-will or God's will?"

Once again, I couldn't "kick against the pricks" as the Lord put it in Acts chapter 9. In these private moments with Him, the Lord confronted me with my struggle and convicted me of an internal, argumentative spirit resisting His Holy Spirit. Suddenly, I plainly saw every spiritual struggle in my heart and how my music choices were a part of the "losing." I saw my sarcastic self-will and how it was connected to my heart influences. I saw my struggles with authority and how certain musical styles were "cheering me on" in rebellion. I saw my tendency to be led more by emotions than by God's Spirit and the connection that fleshly music had in the battle. Suddenly, God connected all the dots for me.

It was as if all the enjoyment, pleasure, and entertainment value of "my music" immediately tasted sick to my heart. I finally heard God's prompting saying, "All this spiritual struggle…and it's only sound! Do you really love all this more than Me?" I was reminded of Jesus' question to Peter in John 21:15, "…lovest thou me more than these?"

In that moment, God won.

I chose to like what He likes—to listen to what He commands—and to honor Him first above my personal tastes and preferences. I finally chose to surrender the circular reasoning and to do what His Word clearly teaches. I chose to stop rationalizing and start obeying.

I wish I could take the pages to recount the changes in my heart and relationship with the Lord since that time. I wish I could share with you how differently my spiritual battles have gone and how my heart responses have changed toward spiritual things.

Suffice it to say, music changed me. The world's music (both secular and Christian) made me edgy in my attitude, argumentative in my spirit, harsh in my nature, and arrogant in my approach to God. Godly music produces a completely different kind of heart. No amount of debate could contradict the personal, spiritual victory of my own surrender to God in this area.

Do you see a correlation between your spiritual struggles and your music? Do you see the connection between your heart attitudes and your musical styles? Your music changes you. It changes your attitude, your spirit, and your lifestyle.

If you are facing the same struggle that I did, simply consider that question, "Is this struggle more about self-will or about God's will?"

The soundtrack of your life is closely related to the spiritual condition of your heart. You cannot separate the two. God's Word is clear. Basic reasoning is clear. Medical and social statistics are clear. Our music always affects us personally and spiritually. God desires to grow you through music and Satan desires to destroy you through it.

Do you value your spiritual health more than you value your personal tastes? I hope so. Do you want your life to be a product of the world or a product of the Holy Spirit? Muzak or God?

If you desire greater victory and growth in your Christian life, then read on. We're about to discover some great news!

"...sing ye praises with understanding."—Psalm 47:7

CHAPTER FIVE

The War of Two Worlds

Understanding the Battle for Your Spirit

Have you ever noticed how subtly and continually Satan attacks your heart, especially regarding the vital relationships that God has placed in your life—your spouse, your children, your parents, your pastor, your church family? It seems like he is constantly trying to divide and destroy these relationships—that he will do anything to prevent them from being healthy and happy.

FEEDING A STUBBORN WILL

Some years ago I sat in a counseling session with a man who had given much of his life to CCM. We had a lengthy, open-hearted discussion about musical style and about whether God really cares about it. During the conversation, there was nothing I could do to convince this man that his music was dangerous and was harming his spiritual life and vital relationships.

It wasn't until after our first two hours of talking that he began to allude to severe struggles in his marriage and home. I was taken aback that this man's marriage was on the brink of dissolution and yet his passion in life was his music! Not only did he care more about his music than his family, but he was oblivious to the connection! The stronghold in his heart was clearly apparent, but he could not see it. His first love was his music, and the rest of his life was coming unraveled as a result.

The same self-will that immerses itself in carnal music, is also fed by that music. Little by little, self-will grows and God's will is pushed aside. As a result, every vital relationship of life is negatively affected. Attitudes change, hearts harden, and strongholds become stronger. Where there should be self-sacrifice there is self-centeredness. Where there should be compassion there is defiance. Where there should be tenderness there is hardness.

Coming back to my personal story—the whole music issue and all the related reasoning and excuses boiled down to a simple battle of wills—my will against God's.

In that struggle, Satan's target was always my heart and my vital relationships. I can trace the struggle of music in my life, and at every point of struggle I can pinpoint strained relationships as well. The battle of wills negatively impacted every area of my heart and life. And friend, it's not just true in me. This is how the spiritual battle works in all of us.

YIELDING MY MEMBERS

Ephesians 6:12 states it this way, "For we wrestle not against flesh and blood, but against principalities, against powers, against the rulers of the darkness of this world, against spiritual wickedness in high places." God says there is an unseen battle raging in all of us—a battle against principalities and powers and rulers of the darkness.

Galatians 5:16–17 references this battle in our flesh, "This I say then, Walk in the Spirit, and ye shall not fulfil the lust of the flesh. For the flesh lusteth against the Spirit, and the Spirit against the flesh: and these are contrary the one to the other: so that ye cannot do the things that ye would." And just a few verses later we're told, "For he that soweth to his flesh shall of the flesh reap corruption; but he that soweth to the Spirit shall of the Spirit reap life everlasting" (Galatians 6:8).

We have been given a daily choice in this battle for control. We must choose to whom we will *yield*. The Bible teaches us to yield our "members"—that is our physical bodies, our hands, our feet, and even our ears—as instruments of righteousness. Take a look:

> "Likewise reckon ye also yourselves to be dead indeed unto sin, but alive unto God through Jesus Christ our Lord. Let not sin therefore reign in your mortal

body, that ye should obey it in the lusts thereof. Neither yield ye your members as instruments of unrighteousness unto sin: but yield yourselves unto God, as those that are alive from the dead, and your members as instruments of righteousness unto God."
—Romans 6:11–13

Paul continues in verse 16, "Know ye not, that to whom ye yield yourselves servants to obey, his servants ye are to whom ye obey; whether of sin unto death, or of obedience unto righteousness?" (Romans 6:16).

The battle for your heart will be won through *yielding*! In other words, if you yield your members (your ears, your mind, your body) to the influences of the world, you can expect to be dominated by such. But if you yield your members to God, your daily battle will be won by His power and your life will reflect His righteousness. The principle is so simple that we overcomplicate it.

How does this pertain to music and what does it have to do with my daily battle between the flesh and the spirit? Think of it this way.

Every time you turn on a TV, you are yielding your members (your eyes, your ears, your mind, and your heart) to those influences. Every time you turn on music or put on headphones, you are yielding your ears, your thoughts, and your heart. If you listen to the world's music, you are yielding your instruments to the flesh. If you listen to godly music, you are yielding to the Spirit of God.

Ultimately, your life will bear the fruit of the seeds you have sown in the heart! Galatians 6:7–8, "Be not deceived; God is not mocked: for whatsoever a man soweth, that shall he also reap. For he that soweth to his flesh shall of the flesh reap corruption; but he that soweth to the Spirit shall of the Spirit reap life everlasting." Your life will display the results of those influences to which you have yielded your members.

YIELDING AGAINST MY WILL

If you struggle with a harmful kind of music that your flesh really likes, it's going to take a heart-shift *within* you before you will make a change.

For example, I used to hate diet soda. I couldn't really even comprehend how anybody could drink Diet Coke. But one day I had a heart-shift. Something I value more than taste registered in my head. I read how much sugar is in a twelve ounce can of Coke and how bad it is for me. Then I stepped on a scale and began to consider what I could do to slow and eventually reverse my "growth"! The first thought was—"go with diet sodas." So, I made a determination. Against the will of my "members"—in particular, my taste buds—I decided to cut out sugary soft drinks. I decided to stop yielding my members to Coke and to start yielding them to Diet Coke.

That was several years ago. It was a simple choice, but wow did my tongue protest! You would almost think it had a will of its own. The Bible calls this a "stronghold." You might say that sugar had a stronghold on my taste buds. Even so, music often has a stronghold in our hearts. But God says, "For the weapons of our warfare are not carnal, but mighty through God to the pulling down of strong holds" (2 Corinthians 10:4).

Against the will of my "members" I have stood by my decision to drink only diet soda. I will tell you the results in the next chapter, but for now get this.

Until I cared more about my health than about my cravings, nothing changed! And until you have a heart-shift and begin to desire God's will more than your own, you will continue to rationalize why "your worldly music" is acceptable.

God says, "yield your members." "Be filled with the Holy Spirit." "Present your body as a living sacrifice." Against your fleshly appetites and carnal desires, by an act of faith—choose to submit to God.

Do you see how our "likes and dislikes" have nothing to do with God's command? We're told to bring our bodies into subjection to His Spirit. We're never told to bring His Spirit into subjection to our desires. We're told to submit our heart cravings to Him. And He promises the result will be "life and peace."

Romans 12:1–2 says, "I beseech you therefore, brethren, by the mercies of God, that ye present your bodies a living sacrifice, holy, acceptable unto God, which is your reasonable service. And be not conformed to this world: but be ye transformed by the renewing of your mind, that ye may prove what is that good, and acceptable, and perfect, will of God."

THE STAKES ARE HIGH

Do you recognize the fierceness of this battle for your spirit? Do you realize how it impacts every detail of your life and relationships?

Your heart for God, your love for your spouse, your care for your children—all of this flows from your heart. Your attitude towards life, towards God, towards His Word, and towards His work is determined by this battle. Your spiritual health and future is at stake here!

The outcome of this battle brings with it thousands of personal implications! The difference between a joyful, peaceful, contented heart and a frustrated, cynical, argumentative heart hangs in the balance! Which do you want? Do you want a growing, healthy, spiritual heart filled with God and His fruit—grace, peace, joy? Or do you want an irritated, confused, unstable, carnally-minded heart that is distant from God and empty spiritually?

Would you like for God to win your battles? Would you like to see greater spiritual victory, more abundant fruit, accelerated spiritual growth, and greater understanding? Would you like to pray more, worry less, see more clearly, and understand more biblically? Would you like to walk in truth and experience God's presence in your life moment by moment?

It begins by desiring these things more than your favorite music style. It begins by having a heart-shift—by placing your will in God's hands. James 4:6–7 says, "But he giveth more grace. Wherefore he saith, God resisteth the proud, but giveth grace unto the humble. Submit yourselves therefore to God. Resist the devil, and he will flee from you."

If you want God and His Spirit to win the daily battle for your heart, keep reading! Cue the best news in the whole book…

CHAPTER SIX

Winning the War

Using God's Great Gift for Transformation

For about four years my taste buds have submitted to my decision to drink only diet sodas. (Not that they've had a choice.) I promised I would tell you the results. Since that time, I've gained five pounds—which sounds bad, but it's actually good when you consider the twenty-five that I would have gained had I not made this change.

But that's not really what I want to share with you. Something changed in my tongue! Over about four months, my taste buds were completely transformed—reprogrammed! My taste buds suffered minimally and eventually decided to go with the rest of my body on this. After just a few months, the "will" of my members gave in to the authority of my decision. From that day until now, I can't stand the overly sweet taste of sugary soda. New appetites and new desires have replaced the old ones.

A RENEWED MIND

In much the same way that my physical tastes were transformed, God desires to supernaturally transform your heart desires and your whole life! He desires to renew your mind and conform you to the image of His Son. Look at this principle in the following verses:

"Therefore if any man be in Christ, he is a new creature: old things are passed away; behold, all things are become new."—2 Corinthians 5:17

"And be not conformed to this world: but be ye transformed by the renewing of your mind..." —Romans 12:2

"And be renewed in the spirit of your mind;" —Ephesians 4:23

"For which cause we faint not; but though our outward man perish, yet the inward man is renewed day by day."—2 Corinthians 4:16

"And have put on the new man, which is renewed in knowledge after the image of him that created him:" —Colossians 3:10

God's plan for winning the battle over your flesh is spiritual *renewal*—complete internal transformation.

Why is this so important? If you get nothing else from this book, get this.

One of God's greatest gifts and most powerful tools in the process of renewing and shaping your "new life in Christ" is spiritual music! This is the real heart of this book—music's power for good and godliness.

Don't misunderstand. Godly music is not a *replacement* for Bible reading, prayer, and right living, but it is a *facilitator* of those things—a powerful contributor to the whole transformation process. It can bring the entire context and emotion of your life into a spiritual environment. Rather than a carnal or ungodly *soundtrack* for your heart, God desires a spiritual one!

We've spent many pages understanding the perversion of Satan, the idolatry of culture, and the conformity of Christians when it comes to carnal music. But now let's flip the coin over! Let's discover God's original intent.

FACILITATING GROWTH

To the same extent that carnal music can conform us into the image of the world, even so *spiritual music* can *transform* us into the *image of Christ*. In the same way that pagan music facilitates a pagan lifestyle, so godly music can facilitate a godly lifestyle. This is why He commands us in Ephesians 5:19 "Speaking to yourselves in psalms and hymns and spiritual songs…" and why Colossians 3 admonishes us to "let the word of Christ dwell" in us through music.

God, in His great love and amazing goodness, has given us a form of communication that accomplishes heart-change enjoyably! (Don't you wish the *dentist* would be so good? Can you imagine actually enjoying a "root canal"?)

Godly music is His gift to you to facilitate your daily walk and spiritual growth in His grace—and in a way that you will greatly enjoy!

Chances are, you've never considered this, so take your time. When you listen to godly music, all of the following is being accomplished at one time in your life:

The Simultaneous Effects of Godly Music

1. *It honors God and His holiness.*
2. *It magnifies His Son.*
3. *It resists Satan.*
4. *It welcomes His Spirit.*
5. *It encourages and strengthens our hearts.*
6. *It facilitates our prayers.*
7. *It places God's peace in our hearts.*
8. *It renews our minds.*
9. *It teaches us God's Word.*
10. *It edifies and encourages others.*
11. *It transforms us into His image.*
12. *It pleases God.*
13. *It gives spiritual context to all of life.*
14. *It gives routine tasks a spiritual element.*
15. *It brings joy to the heart.*
16. *It witnesses of Christ to lost men.*
17. *It sets one apart from the world.*
18. *It sets our affections upon God.*
19. *It brings rest to your spirit.*
20. *It establishes our hearts in the faith.*

And that's just the short list! Name one other activity that accomplishes so much spiritually with so little effort! What a great God! And today's modern technology only makes godly music that much more accessible to the surrendered Christian! By merely pressing a button we can experience spiritual growth and life-transformation! What a great use of an iPod!

OVERWHELMINGLY POSITIVE NEWS

You see, the message of this book is *good news*! It's not primarily about what you *can't* listen to or what you must give up! Look at the overwhelming, positive aspects of godly music. Look what you stand to *gain* if you will surrender your heart and yield your members to righteousness. The *rewards* are *immeasurable*!

In contrast, the risks of self-will are great. By standing against God's will in this matter, you face two great dangers—the danger of missing the abundant spiritual growth and blessings that godly music will facilitate, as well as the danger of all the damage that carnal music will bring upon your heart and home!

Remember—music *changes* you! If you are truly saved and Christ is in your heart, somewhere deep within, you long to grow in faith. You long for daily spiritual victory. You long for the presence of God, the blessings of His favor, and the knowledge that He is pleased with your life. You long to know that you are becoming more like Him.

Godly music is one of God's greatest gifts in accomplishing all this and much more in your heart. And all He requires of you is that you *yield*—that you give in to His will—that you "let" it happen! Colossians 3:16 says, "Let the word of Christ dwell in you richly in all wisdom; teaching and admonishing one another in psalms and hymns and spiritual songs, singing with grace in your hearts to the Lord."

This is God's primary purpose in music—*His glory and your transformation*, not your entertainment. J.S. Bach said, "The aim and final end of all music should be none other than the glory of God and the refreshment of the soul." Throughout God's Word we see music used as a tool of worship, a tool of renewal, and a tool of spiritual growth.

How can we "let the Word of Christ dwell" in us? How can we "pray without ceasing"? How can we "rejoice in the Lord always"? How do we bring every thought "into captivity" and let our minds dwell on the things listed in Philippians 4:8? I believe Paul and Silas answered these questions in the Philippian jail—by yielding your members (your ears, your voice, and your whole body) to godly music! And God answers our questions over and over again in His Word:

> "Sing unto him, sing psalms unto him, talk ye of all his wondrous works."—1 Chronicles 16:9

> "Sing unto the LORD, all the earth; shew forth from day to day his salvation."—1 Chronicles 16:23

"Praise the LORD with harp: sing unto him with the psaltery and an instrument of ten strings. Sing unto him a new song; play skillfully with a loud noise."
—Psalm 33:2–3

"Sing unto the LORD, O ye saints of his, and give thanks at the remembrance of his holiness."—Psalm 30:4

"My heart is fixed, O God, my heart is fixed: I will sing and give praise."—Psalm 57:7

"I will praise thee, O Lord, among the people: I will sing unto thee among the nations."—Psalm 57:9

"And he hath put a new song in my mouth, even praise unto our God: many shall see it, and fear, and shall trust in the LORD."—Psalm 40:3

God designed music with an amazing power to change your life for the better! It will transform your heart, strengthen your home, establish your spirit, and renew your mind. But it does require an act of faith.

You must choose to go with God. You must surrender your selfish desires and *yield*.

When you take this step of faith, something miraculous will happen. God has prewired your spirit for a pretty amazing transformation, but you will only experience it if you trust Him first! Let's find out what happens when my will dies and His wins.

CHAPTER SEVEN

A New Set of Taste Buds

Experiencing the Wonderful Results of Trusting God

Wouldn't it be great if God would flip a switch and change your desires! Think how easy the Christian life would be if He would just snap His fingers and remove our fleshly appetites—if He could end the battle against sin by instantly changing our desires completely.

He could, but that would defeat His eternal purpose. That would preempt your acting in "faith"—which is required to please Him.

He has a different plan in mind. It's not about flipping a switch, but rather renewing a mind. It's not the snap of His fingers, but rather the process of His Spirit—and He's planning for it to take your entire lifetime. "Being confident of this very thing, that he which hath begun a good work in you will perform it until the day of Jesus Christ" (Philippians 1:6).

SUGAR FOR YOUR SOUL

The really great news is this—God does intend to change your desires. He intends to take away old appetites and awaken new ones that lie dormant in your "new nature"! Yes, if you are saved, these new appetites are already in you and need only to be given a chance to thrive! God says it this way in Romans 7:18, "For I know that in me (that is, in my flesh) dwelleth no good thing: for to will is present with me; but how to perform that which is good I find not." And He promises, "Delight thyself also in the LORD; and he shall give thee the desires of thine heart" (Psalm 37:4).

Your musical tastes are very much like my taste bud story. If you are hooked on the wrong music, like sugar for your soul, then it will be difficult to imagine listening to anything different. In fact, in your nature, you are probably somewhat repulsed by the bitter taste of godly music—much like I was by the taste of Diet Coke.

Yet, if you are willing to value your spiritual health and growth more than you value your taste, God can do something amazing. He can replace your carnal desires with spiritual desires. He can renew your mind. He can take away your taste for wrong music and replace it with a taste for godly music.

How do I know this to be true? First, because that is His promise in Scripture—to renew our minds and transform our lives. Second, because this is what I personally have experienced.

You will discover that "it's only sound!" There's no sense damaging your heart and home over it, especially when "what you like today" could change in a short time if you give God a chance.

SURRENDER FOR YOUR HEART

I'm talking about old-fashioned, Bible-based surrender. I'm talking about losing the battle of wills. Pray as Jesus prayed, "thy will be done" (Matthew 26:42). Pray with the psalmist, "Teach me to do thy will; for thou art my God: thy spirit is good; lead me into the land of uprightness" (Psalm 143:10).

Ask the Lord to search your heart and your music library and reveal to you what is worldly. The Holy Spirit in your conscience will not have a problem doing this. He communicates clearly to a sincerely yielded heart. He will expose music that is "war-like"—music that is conformed to this world and of this world. He will expose music that is beat-driven, sensual, carnal, and fleshly. Be willing to lose this music—both secular and CCM—for your own spiritual health.

At this point, your taste buds will revolt! You will think things like, "I've invested all this money into this collection!" "But I really like this group!" "This really can't be all that bad!" "I'd better save this just in case!" A spiritual battle will rage within you. Satan will not give up his stronghold easily. Yield to God anyway. Do what you *know* in your heart is *right* before God. Choose God above your taste buds!

A SIX-MONTH TEST

Then go on a spiritual diet. Replace your worldly music with that which is "above reproach." Build a music library that honors the Lord and contains music of "grace"—psalms, hymns, and spiritual songs. Choose songs that are strong in melody, positive in harmony (as opposed to dissonant or distorted), and light in rhythm and beat. Choose songs that speak to your spirit and not to your flesh.

I warn you—you will not enjoy this music at first, especially if it's vastly different from what you've been enjoying in the flesh. This will not be fun at first, but it will be healthy, spiritually speaking!

Then, commit to God for six months. That is my proposal. Go on a carnal music fast for six months! Decide that you will listen to nothing but spiritual music—that which is beyond question pleasing to Christ and inviting to His Holy Spirit—the kind of music that is without a doubt holy and godly and not conformed to this world.

I dare you to do this. You will be delighted with what happens in your heart.

First, for several days or weeks, you will dislike what you are hearing. What a blessing! And by the way, *not* listening to music isn't an option! You can't just "stop listening to all music." That defeats the purpose of what God wants to do in your life. For the test to work, you must intentionally listen to godly music, whether you like it or not.

As you listen to this new music (that you dislike), stop and think about it. Consider the truth that it is speaking. Consider the emotions that it is creating. Think about how you are responding in your body, in your mind, in your emotions. Consider whether this is a spiritual or a carnal response that the music is producing. Even though you don't like it (in your flesh), look beyond that—after all, it's only sound. Think about what it's *doing to you.*

AN AMAZING TRANSFORMATION

Something subtle and powerful will begin to happen within you, by God's grace. You will change. God's power will begin to renew you. It will first show up as you think about what you are hearing, even though you don't particularly "like it." Somewhere deep within you, the Holy Spirit will resonate with the good work that is beginning in your heart. You will find joy in the knowledge that something good is happening inside.

Then over time, you will actually begin to *like* and eventually *love* the music that God loves! You will love it because it makes you love Christ more. You will love it because it pleases Him. You will love it because it feeds your spirit and not your flesh. You will love it because it restores your soul and strengthens your heart! With every passing month, you will find another hundred reasons to love godly music and what it produces in your heart.

Eventually, you will look back and see the spiritual distance you have traveled—you won't ever want to go back! You won't believe how strong your worldly music was in your heart, and you won't believe the good grace of God and all that He has changed within you. You will find more delight in *spiritual growth* than you ever found in carnal music!

And, eventually you will abhor what once so powerfully entertained you. Yes, eventually, you will have a great disdain for the music you once loved and the world you once followed. You will think, "Wow... what I would have missed if I hadn't surrendered in this area of my life!"

Those old desires will die a brief but miserable death only to give way to new, wholesome, godly desires. As you nurture your spirit through godly music, you will be able to say with the psalmist, "I delight to do thy will, O my God: yea, thy law is within my heart" (Psalm 40:8).

Music changes you. It does something to you. Carnal music feeds carnality; spiritual music feeds spirituality. The two don't mix. Let God give you a taste for the spiritual, and you will love what it will produce in your heart.

Six months—go ahead, give it a shot. What do you have to lose? Give God the chance to change your taste buds. You'll never regret it!

"My meditation of him shall be sweet: I will be glad in the LORD."—Psalm 104:34

CHAPTER EIGHT

Staying on the Offensive
Practical Ideas for Your Music Choices

As we turn the final corner on this book, thank you for staying with it this long. Whether or not you're struggling with the wrong music, I appreciate your desire to seek and understand God's will.

We've come a long way. We've seen a lot of Scripture and heard from many who believe strongly in the power of music. I'd like to close with some practical suggestions that you can implement today to capitalize on God's gift of good music. These ideas will serve to protect your heart and home, and they will serve to grow them as well!

These are just my suggestions—things I practice in my own life and home—based upon what we've learned. Consider them:

1. Intentionally fill your life and home with godly music. This will take some planning and maybe some investment, but it will change the whole dynamic of your family relationships. In the morning, at dinner time, and in the evening, turn off the TV and turn on godly music.

2. Choose the best rather than what "might be acceptable." Raise your standard and be ultra safe. Take the high road. When in doubt, don't. Rather than asking, "What's wrong with this music?" ask, "Is this music as right as it could be?" I believe this thinking pleases the Lord more than, "God, let me get as close to the world as I can!"

3. Turn down or "off" any wrong music in any form of entertainment. Have you noticed how Satan sneaks carnal music into every sports program, every video game, and every family movie? He wants young hearts. While I'm not suggesting that you ban all these things from your life or home completely, I am suggesting that you use the remote control to block it out. Don't sit there passively and let this music impact you. Take control of what you allow into your heart. For many years now, in our home, we turn off any carnal music from any source—TV commercials, family films, video games, etc. This will go a long way toward developing healthy appetites in yourself and others.

4. Seek to avoid wrong music in public places when possible. This is tough, but not impossible. You can't always control what is played in public, but you can control how long you stay, where you sit, and whether or not to say something to the management. Some stores are dominated by driving, carnal music. I would try to avoid them or at least minimize my time there. Some stores are flexible and respond to a simple request from customers to turn it down or off. Frankly, there are some places that we refuse to take our children—even to buy a T-shirt—simply because of the perverted music and videos that are playing in public.

5. Parents, don't buy the lie that "kids are just going to listen to this." I'm amazed at the carnality that we condone as Christians in the name of "youth." Teach your teenager the dangers of wrong music and the value of good, and help them develop healthy appetites. They can handle it! More importantly, teach them the biblical value of submission to God.

6. Provide spiritual alternatives. I'm for godly music. I need it personally. I want my children to have access to right music, and I want them to listen to it. It's up to you to combat the world's influence with healthy alternatives. Buy an iPod or a portable player and make its use conditional upon godly music! Control what goes on it and, if you're a parent, help your teenager manage the content. Get involved in leading your children through this process and fight the fight with them. Expect the devil to fight them in this area, and help them win the battle.

7. Educate others with biblical understanding. This can't merely be a "because I said so" issue in your home or with friends and relations. The world's pressure is too strong. Your children and those you influence need a principled foundation for "why" they shouldn't listen to certain music. They need to grow in spiritual understanding and awareness of music's power and presence around them. Don't be afraid to put some positive, loving pressure on friends. Parent, don't be afraid to clearly articulate the "why" behind your rules. You'll know you're starting to win the battle when your children start using the remote control on their own to mute or change the channel from wrong music.

8. Avoid worldly music in "Christian" disguises. There is much music today being offered in the name of Christ that is merely a duplicate of the world. Some popular animated children's series are merely MTV take-offs. Most of the CCM movement, behind the scenes, is just a carbon copy of what Nashville and Hollywood are producing. One look at the *private music collections* of these popular CCM artists, writers, publishers, and producers would reveal the truth of what I'm saying. (Yes, I am an eyewitness.) They personally listen to and mimic the world's music. They study the world and then emulate it. God's mandate is that we study Christ and emulate Him! For them it's a business—primarily about money. They market what sells, not what transforms. You are an "end user"—a dollar sign.

9. Parents, start early with young children. Worldly appetites enlarge themselves with time and they are much easier dealt with in a young heart. Help your children develop an early appreciation for spiritual music. Don't give them access to music and portable players without your direct involvement in what they hear. Early in our home, my boys came to understand that I, as their loving father, own several things: their clothes, their hair, and their entertainment. We settled that years ago. Now as teenagers, they're just good with it. No questions. No fights. That's just the way it is—and God has blessed it.

10. Don't become judgmental or overly obsessive. If one thing is true about this issue, it's that not all believers are always going to see eye to eye. We're going to split hairs differently in some ways. Please don't get pharisaical about this issue. Don't become arrogant, pious, or condescending towards people who don't draw the line exactly how you draw it. Remember, God resists pride as much as He resists carnality. And don't think I'm saying that you shouldn't go out in public places or eat at restaurants. Be aware, be cautious, be protective, but don't be proud or judgmental.

The question I'm asked the most is, "What kind of music is godly?" The problem with this question is that we could fill volumes trying to dissect every one of thousands of styles and nuances of music and still not cover all of them. It's an open-ended question—and as soon as it's answered for "today" there are fourteen new genres of music tomorrow that need to be addressed. For this reason, I've tried to avoid getting bogged down in the endless cycle of inspecting every kind or style.

Rather than try to define my concept of worldly, I believe the greatest, most sincere question you can ask the Holy Spirit in this matter is, *"Lord, what is this music doing to me, and does it please You?"* I truly believe that He will answer that question. He will let you know what is spiritual and what is sensual, what is godly and what is angry, what is transforming you into the image of Christ and what is conforming you to culture. He will guide you away from rebellion and into submission. He will guide you away from the flesh and into the Spirit.

Choose to listen to that which pleases God first! Jesus said, "…for I do always those things that please him" (John 8:29).

We've seen many biblical principles that can guide your decision. Allow me to summarize some guidelines from God's Word.

Guiding Principles for Godly Music:

1. *It should not sound like "war in the camp."* (Exodus 32:17–18)

2. *It should sound like praising.* (2 Chronicles 5:13)

3. *It should be different from the world.* (Romans 12:2)

4. *It should be psalms, hymns, and spiritual songs.*
   (Ephesians 5:19)

5. *It should be "singing with grace." (Colossians 3:16)*

6. *It should be a new song (different from the world).*
   (Psalm 40:3)

7. *It should facilitate the filling of God's Holy Spirit.*
   (Ephesians 5:18–19)

8. *It should instruct me in God's Word. (Colossians 3:16)*

9. *It should be spiritual, as opposed to fleshly or carnal*
   (melody led rather than beat driven).
   (Ephesians 5:19–20)

10. *It should facilitate God's transforming work and*
    combat the world's conforming work.
    (Romans 12:1–2)

11. *It should witness to others of Christ. (Psalm 40:3)*

12. *It should repel evil spirits and welcome God's Spirit.*
    (1 Samuel 16:23)

13. *It should strengthen my life. (Psalm 81:1)*

14. *It should be pleasant. (Psalm 81:2)*

15. *It should be joyful. (Psalm 100:1)*

16. *It should be understandable. (Psalm 47:7; 1 Corinthians 14:15)*

17. *It should let God's peace rule in my heart. (Colossians 3:15–16)*

18. *It should express thanks. (Psalm 100:4)*

19. *It should produce godly emotions. (Isaiah 65:14)*

20. *It should produce spiritual fruit in my life. (Romans 6:16)*

21. *It should help to protect my heart. (Proverbs 4:23)*

22. *It should worship and extol my God. (Psalm 29:2)*

23. *It should be orderly and not of confusion. (1 Corinthians 14:10, 14:33)*

24. *It should glorify God. (1 Corinthians 10:31)*

This is just a brief glance at what could be pages upon pages of guiding principles for music and for life. Trying to be exhaustive in this matter would be futile. God's Word is clear, if we will trust Him and obey.

"Speaking to yourselves in psalms and hymns and spiritual songs, singing and making melody in your heart to the Lord."—Ephesians 5:19

Conclusion

In these pages I've tried to appeal to the deep spiritual desires of your heart. I've tried to set aside the typical music banter that runs Christians in argumentative circles, and I've tried to get you thinking about what your music is doing to you—on a spiritual level. I've tried to turn your heart toward spiritual things and away from carnal things.

By now, I hope you distrust your fleshly desires. I pray that you value your heart. Hollywood and Nashville certainly don't.

The music you listen to changes you. Who do you want to be? Who do you desire to be like? A pop artist? A CCM artist? How about Jesus?

In closing, I want to remind you that this is about God's process of growth in your heart. I cannot mandate your choices, nor would I desire such. The Bible is clear that godly music is a part of God's process of spiritual transformation, and one look at secular or CCM culture reveals that the opposite is taking place—conformity to the world.

Friend, I realize that there are good people, who deeply love Jesus Christ, who personally land all over this issue. I do not question their sincerity, their love for God, or their heart motives. I realize that our music choices are but one facet of this wonderful life that we call "Christian." I am not at war with those who disagree with me. I'm just urgently burdened that we have given one of God's best gifts over to the world, the flesh, and the devil, and I pray that you will consider the principles we've studied. You have much to gain through godly music.

God would do a renewing work in our lives and in our churches if we would return to godly musical styles. Many may come to Christ if we would exalt *Him* more than our *flesh*. The unsaved are often looking with interest at Christianity—wondering if there really is any substance to what we believe. Too often, they see a mirror image of themselves rather than the image of Christ. I believe they hunger to see a difference—a new life, a new song, a new hope.

May God give us the courage to do what is right, both personally and corporately.

Whether you set this book down agreeing or disagreeing, you must walk away with at least this much— "my music is changing me." Let that sink in. Dwell on that thought. Perhaps the Holy Spirit of God will burden you enough with it that you will eventually be compelled to make a change.

From this moment forward, I hope you will never think of music the same way again. Every time you hear music, I pray the Holy Spirit will prompt this thought— "this is changing me!"

Look beyond the trivial entertainment value.

Think about what it is *doing to you*.

Thank you for reading. Thank you for investigating God's principles. I pray these words will compel you to choose spiritual music and that your heart, your life, and your home will benefit for many years from the wonderful, positive power of godly music. I pray that your relationship with Christ will be stronger and closer because of what you hear.

Don't just listen to what you like. Listen to what is right. Eventually God will help you like what is right. Choose to follow truth over your emotions.

Music matters! After reading these pages, I pray that you agree. Go discover how godly music can change your life!

Yield your members to God.
And may God bless you as you do!

"Thou wilt keep him in perfect peace, whose mind is stayed on thee: because he trusteth in thee."—Isaiah 26:3

Index of Scriptures

For questions, comments, or additional copies of this minibook, please contact us:

WRITE   Striving Together Publications
4020 E. Lancaster Blvd.
Lancaster, CA 93535

CALL   800.201.7748

EMAIL   info@strivingtogether.com

GO ONLINE   www.strivingtogether.com

Suggested Reading for Further Research

Each of the following books offers principles and concepts helpful to a study on the subject of the effects of music. While one may not agree with every suggestion in each book, they are worth reading for any serious student of this subject.

Christian Resources:

Music in the Balance—Dr. Frank Garlock
A Song in Your Heart—Dr. Mike Zachary
Why I Left the Contemporary Christian Music Movement—Dan Lucarini
The Battle for Christian Music—Tim Fisher
Oh Be Careful Little Ears—Kimberly Smith
Let Those Who Have Ears to Hear—Kimberly Smith
Music and Morals—Kimberly Smith
Worship in the Melting Pot—Peter Masters

Secular Resources:

The Closing of the American Mind—Allan Bloom
Amusing Ourselves To Death—Neil Postman
The Marketing of Evil—David Kupelian

About the Author

Cary Schmidt serves as an associate pastor at Lancaster Baptist Church and an instructor at West Coast Baptist College. He leads the student ministries, music ministry, and the media and publications ministries of the church. His other books include *Life Quest; Discover Your Destiny; Hook, Line and Sinker; and Done.*

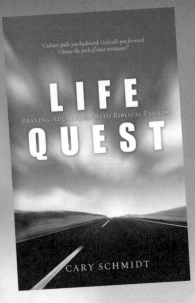

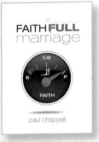

Visit us online

strivingtogether.com

dailyintheword.org

wcbc.edu

lancasterbaptist.org